Popcorn

by Patrick Evans-Hylton

SASQUATCH BOOKS
SEATTLE

Printed in Singapore by Star Standard Industries Pte Ltd

Published by Documentary Book Publishing

15 14 13 12 11 10 09 08   9 8 7 6 5 4 3 2 1

Cover design: Rosebud Eustace

Cover and interior photographs: Lara Ferroni

Interior design and composition: Rosebud Eustace

Library of Congress Cataloging-in-Publication Data is available.

  ISBN-13: 978-0-9821188-0-1
  ISBN-10: 0-9821188-0-5

Documentary Book Publishing

119 South Main Street, Suite 400

Seattle, WA 98104

(206) 467-4300

Contents

Introduction

It may be hard to believe there could be a cookbook about nothing other than popcorn, but here it is.

Consider that freshly popped corn is, in its unadulterated state, a perfect snack food. It is high in fiber. It is low in calories. It has no fat or sodium. And while its flavor profile is pleasant, it is muted.

This makes popcorn an excellent platform for a vast array of treatments, from adding savory seasonings to touches of sweetness. Movie-style popcorn dripping in butter and loaded with salt is so 1950s. Today's popcorn sheds its June Cleaver image and emerges with bold flavors to knock the socks off Ward.

Look no further than this collection to uncover all the most current flavors: spicy Indian, sugar and cinnamon, fresh herbs such as rosemary and basil, classic combinations like peanut butter and chocolate. How about a large, half-caf, skinny mocha latte with hazelnut?

Don't have time for a big production? Purchase an oil mister or a never-used spray bottle; use it to spritz popcorn with olive oil, or even the likes of tequila, for a quick-and-easy flavor boost as well as a moisture platform before tossing with a few dry seasonings.

Popcorn also is a great addition to many main dishes. It's so versatile: it can be ground and used as a filler in crab cakes, a coating on scallops, or to make amazing "pop"corn bread.

The possibilities are endless—we've easily thought up a mere 60 popcorn recipes. How many more will you create?

A Brief History of Popcorn

In the beginning, there was popcorn.

True, it wasn't quite the same as the popcorn we know now. It wasn't popped in a machine, spewing popped kernels—also known as flakes—into a big bowl, ready for melted butter and savory seasonings. But it seems popcorn caught many an eye, even as far back as some 5,000 years ago, making popping kernels one of the first uses of wild and cultivated corn.

Kernels and ears at least 2,000 years old have been found in an Arizona cave. The corn was popped by placing kernels in a bowl with sand and heating it all over a fire. As the sand warmed, the kernels popped and rose to the top. More than likely it was then ground and made into a type of porridge.

Corn was part of the Native American diet then, too: flint corn was parched then eaten, and field corn was ground then made into breadlike edibles. Popcorn was also important to Aztecs, Peruvians, and other native cultures.

English settlers became fond of popcorn after they were introduced to it by Native Americans, who ate the popcorn out of hand, ground it for making gruel, made popcorn beer with it, and used it for jewelry and decoration. The colonists called it popped corn, parching corn, and rice corn, and a common practice was to serve it with sugar and cream as a breakfast cereal.

When the plow became widely used in the mid-nineteenth century, larger areas of corn fields became possible, and popcorn as a snack really caught on. It was sold all over town by vendors on the street, at fairs and exhibitions, and in parks. At first the kernels were popped in wire baskets held over an open flame; by 1893 Charles Cretors had introduced a mobile machine that is recognized as the first mechanical popper.

Popcorn became very popular at sporting events, and in 1912 it began a lasting love affair with the silver screen. Around the same time, a confection from F. W. Rueckheim and his brother, Louis, combining caramel-coated popcorn and peanuts was introduced: Cracker Jack.

The Great Depression was a boom time for popcorn, which was seen as one of the few affordable luxuries during this time. Another boost came during World War II, when candy production went into a tailspin as sugar was sent to American troops overseas and was rationed at home; Americans consumed three times as much popcorn as during peacetime.

In the 1950s popcorn fell out of favor—as did motion pictures—when America became enamored with television. Fortunately, it wasn't too long before people realized they could make and eat popcorn at home.

The latest and greatest boon for the snack treat was the advent of microwave popcorn in the 1980s. Throw a bag in the oven, hit a few buttons, and enjoy. (Well, enjoy if you could get past the overly salty, sickening imitation butter flavor with the chemical aftertaste, that is.)

Once again, popcorn is reaching a new frontier. As Americans spend more time at home, popcorn is a healthy, quick, and easy snack. And as home cooks become more and more interested in gourmet and global flavors, the blank canvas that is freshly popped corn is a prime choice for all sorts of tasty and tempting toppings and preparations.

Types of Popcorn

There are a handful of basic corn varieties, but only one of these will make popcorn. The shell, or pericarp, is especially hard on popcorn kernels, which allows a great deal of steam to build up from the heated moisture inside before it finally explodes. The "pop" turns the kernel inside out, and the moisture floats away as a puff of steam. Other types of corn just can't measure up.

Within the popcorn family, there are several variations. Popcorn is available in a variety of colors, from the familiar white and yellow to red, black, or gold. You may also come across "hull-less" kernels: although every popcorn kernel has a hull, these modified varieties were developed to make the hull virtually undetectable. All popcorn pops in one of two basic shapes: butterfly and mushroom.

The butterfly flake is spread out and looks somewhat like it has wings. This shape is good for capturing dry toppings like salt, herbs, and spices. It is also good for providing a surface area to hold compound flavored butters and oils. Typically, butterfly flakes are deemed more delicate and palate pleasing.

Mushroom flakes, on the other hand, are round and compact; they are well adapted for use with candy or caramelized toppings. They are also an ideal component of popcorn balls, since they lack the wings that frequently break off with this type of handling.

Sometimes, however, life gives you mushrooms when you want butterflies. A single cob of popcorn may contain both butterfly and mushroom kernels, although hybrid kernels exist that can produce 100 percent of either variety.

So, when shopping for kernels to pop, what should you look for?

Today, there is a wide assortment of popcorn available. Some companies advertise their kernels as "gourmet." Others are produced in Amish country in a variety of colors, including midnight blue, red, purple, and black. Still others are generic store brands. Some kernels are hybrid breeds to impart specific flake shapes or other Frankencorn properties.

The only way to determine what the best popcorn is for you is by sampling the many varieties. Believe it or not, popcorn is a lot like wine. It picks up some of its characteristics from the *terroir*—a mix of the soil and climate where it is grown. There are also plenty of cheap popcorns on the market, like your wine-in-a-box, as well as some real thoroughbreds (often with steep prices accompanying them).

Most of the time, the lower-grade corn is shipped off for use in lesser-known and store brands. If you start with popcorn of a moderate price and a recognizable company name, you are likely to be pleased with its quality. Invest in a good, airtight glass container to store kernels and keep the container in a cool, dry place.

Why Corn Pops

The tiny golden nugget that is a popcorn kernel consists of a small drop of liquid tucked inside a circle of soft starch (or endosperm). As the kernel—and some 1,599 of his friends if you pop a full cup—heats up, the water expands. Steam starts building up when the kernel is heated to around 212°F.

Eventually the hard surface (or hull) around the soft starch gives way, exploding as if in a pressure cooker. The soft starch inflates and turns into a very hot, gel-like glob as steam at a temperature of 347°F filters into the air.

This popping may seem to be a pretty simple feat, but it actually requires just the right amount of moisture in the kernel (13½ to 14 percent is ideal) and the correct amount of heat. Too much or too little of either, and the results are disappointing, at the least.

Popping Methods

How do I pop thee? Let me count the ways. There are four basic methods for getting those little kernels to explode, creating a lighter-than-air snack experience:

Stovetop Poppers

This is the way kernels were popped in the majority of households up until the advent in the 1960s of automatic poppers and microwaves. Although commercial machines powered by steam, gas, and later, electricity, took up residence at fairs, parks, and expositions, when folks wanted to "flake out" at home, they popped their kernels in a pot on the stove.

Many home cooks used cast-iron poppers mail-ordered from the likes of Montgomery Ward and Sears, Roebuck and Co. Others put kernels in a deep stockpot and popped the kernels in butter, oil, or lard. Then in 1959, Fred

Mennen of Indiana developed Jiffy Pop: an aluminum foil pan filled with kernels and oil, covered with a folded aluminum foil lid that puffed up and expanded as the popcorn popped.

Today, success can still be achieved with stovetop popping and, in fact, some recipes work best using this method. Watch for notes on this method throughout the book and see the basic stovetop popcorn recipe on page 15.

Mechanical Poppers

In their early years, home poppers were only as advanced as a person's arm was strong: either a pan or hand crank had to be operated to create movement of the kernels. It wasn't until the 1960s that home machines powered by electricity were commonplace. Some used oil and a motorized stirring rod; the alternative—popular in the health-conscious '70s—used hot air and no oil to flake the kernels.

Generally, air-popped corn works best with recipes like popcorn balls and caramel corn. The flake is dry and ready to take on sugary, sticky substances. Kernels popped in oil or another fat are better for recipes calling for additional wet toppings like butter or sprayed liquids. Dry seasonings also work well as they cling to the oil residue on the flakes.

There are a couple of things to keep in mind when selecting a mechanical popper:

- Do you want a popper that works without adding oil or butter? Search out an air popper. You simply pour kernels into the machine, plug it in, and let the hot air do its job. Place a bowl under the spout to catch the falling flakes and snack away.

- Are you interested in using a little oil, or the ability to automatically melt butter as the kernels pop? With an electric popper you just add oil and some kernels, plug in the machine, and watch it go. A mechanized bar sweeps around inside the popper to keep the popcorn moving. Butter, placed in the slotted reservoir above the main compartment, melts from the heat of the escaping steam and coats the popcorn below. In some models, the dome flips over and doubles as a serving bowl.

Homemade Microwave Popcorn

In general, kernels popped in a microwave oven are considered to make the best popcorn because they are heated from the inside out. The moisture in the kernel heats more quickly than in traditional poppers, producing a stronger burst and larger, more tender flakes.

There are two sure methods for popping kernels in the microwave: using a high-density, microwave-safe plastic bowl shaped for heat convection that has a plastic lid with vents, or using a clean paper bag. The bowl has the advantage of being slightly more environmentally friendly—no paper waste. It can also pop kernels without any added oil or butter (whereas kernels place in a paper bag should be lightly coated).

A good old-fashioned brown paper lunch bag will work just as well though. See the basic recipe for lunch-bag popcorn on page 16.

Store-Bought Microwave Popcorn

These compact bags come with all sorts of additions along with the popcorn kernels: solidified oil, artificial flavors, and an overabundance of salt. Recently the chronic condition *bronchiolitis obliterans*, also known as "popcorn lung," became associated with this unhealthy version of the snack. The illness, which can significantly diminish breathing capacity, is reportedly caused by inhaling chemical fumes such as diacetyl (an imitation butter flavoring) from the popcorn bags.

So repeat after me: "I will not eat store-bought microwave popcorn." It is easy enough to make fresh, chemical-free popcorn in the microwave with your own paper bag.

The Basics

Popcorn is best made according to loose estimations and subject to creativity and personal taste. Think of these recipes more as guidelines than as strict formulas.

Start with the basic information that three tablespoons of popcorn kernels equal about one quart of popped corn—sometimes more, sometimes less depending on the method of popping as well as the brand and age of the kernels. The two recipes that immediately follow offer the simplest instructions for your basic bowl of popcorn.

Also realize that some recipes may not want to cooperate in humid conditions. Or perhaps your oven runs hotter than the ones we used to test the recipes. The best part of these potential variances is that, as a rule, you can eat your mistakes.

I recommend you invest in an inexpensive muslin bag (or alternatively, a cheesecloth bag) in which to shake and coat your popcorn. You can simply wash, dry, and reuse it for each new batch. These bags are widely available online and at stores that sell home-brewing supplies. The key is that they be "food grade" and quite large—a five-pound capacity is best. Bags with a drawstring are a real benefit, but a drawstring is really more of a convenience than a necessity.

Also, many cooks prefer the pure salt flavor of coarse kosher and sea salts, and I recommend using them to season your popcorn. However, if you find yourself at home with only regular table salt, shake away.

Another note: You will see references to "popcorn crumbs" in several recipes. This is merely freshly popped corn placed in a food processor and ground to the consistency of coarse bread crumbs.

Any other questions? No? Good—now get popping!

Popcorn in a Pot

This basic recipe is ideal for your popcorn repertoire. It is the perfect popping method for most of the recipes in this book—especially when they call for a powdered or finely ground mixture to coat the popcorn hot off the stovetop. Adding the seasonings immediately to the freshly popped corn will enhance your snacking experience.

You should experiment with a variety of oils—canola, vegetable, olive, coconut, corn, peanut, grape seed, sunflower. Each one imparts a slightly different flavor. Which do you like the best?

The ratio of kernels to oil here will yield one, two, and four quarts of popcorn, respectively. Simply adjust the size of your pot for the preferred yield.

MAKES 1 QUART	1 tablespoon oil of your choice
	3 tablespoons popcorn kernels
	1 teaspoon salt

MAKES 2 QUARTS	2 tablespoons oil of your choice
	6 tablespoons popcorn kernels
	2 teaspoons salt

MAKES 4 QUARTS	¼ cup oil of your choice
	¾ cup popcorn kernels
	1 tablespoon plus 1 teaspoon salt

- In a deep pot, heat the oil over medium heat. Add a few kernels to the pot. Once they pop, add the remaining kernels and shake the pot until they cover the bottom of the pot evenly. Cover the pot and shake intermittently until the popping slows to 5 seconds between pops. Remove the pot from the heat and transfer the popcorn to a large bowl. Season with the salt immediately, tossing gently to coat.

Lunch-Bag Popcorn

Use this method to make popcorn in a microwave oven without giving in to the artificially flavored and chemically propped-up commercial stuff you might find in the grocery store. Use a regular brown paper lunch bag as the cooking vessel. Depending on the size of your microwave and paper bag, we don't recommend you use this method to make more than two quarts of popcorn at a time. Although this recipe calls for a small amount of oil, you can omit it all together if you wish.

MAKES 1 QUART

3 tablespoons popcorn kernels
1 teaspoon canola oil

- In a small bowl, combine the kernels and oil; stir to coat. Transfer the kernels to a clean paper bag, fold over the top of the bag ½ inch, and then fold again another ½ inch. Seal the bag with a small strip of cellophane tape. Place the bag in the microwave, folded side up, and cook on high heat for 2 to 3 minutes, or until there are 5 seconds between pops.

Savory

Lemon-Pepper Popcorn

A tart and piquant snack, this popcorn in all its lemony-pepper goodness showcases a unique teaming of flavors. Enjoy this sophisticated, savory variety out of hand paired with a slightly buttery Chardonnay, or used as croutons in a Caesar salad or floated on top of a creamy tomato soup.

MAKES 4 QUARTS

4 quarts freshly popped corn
½ tablespoon lemon zest
2 teaspoons finely ground black pepper
¼ teaspoon salt
2 teaspoons freshly squeezed lemon juice
2 tablespoons olive oil

- Put the popcorn in a large, clean paper bag or a washable muslin bag. In a small bowl, combine the lemon zest, pepper, and salt. In a separate bowl, whisk together the lemon juice and oil.

- Drizzle the lemon juice mixture over the popcorn, fold over the top of the bag, and shake until the popcorn is coated and moist. Sprinkle the lemon zest mixture over the popcorn, fold over the top of the bag, and shake a few times to coat.

Unpopped kernels are also known as "old maids."

Green Tea and Sea Salt Popcorn

The grassy flavor of green tea marries with the complementary tastes of lemon zest and ginger and is topped off with coarse sea salt to create a unique snack. Green tea is purported to have many health benefits, but we just know we love the taste.

MAKES 4 QUARTS

4 quarts freshly popped corn
1 tablespoon green tea leaves, finely ground, or
   Matcha green tea powder
1 teaspoon lemon zest
½ teaspoon ground ginger
1½ teaspoons sea salt plus additional for serving
3 tablespoons canola oil

- Put the popcorn in a large, clean paper bag or a washable muslin bag. In a small bowl, combine the tea leaves, lemon zest, ginger, and salt.

- Drizzle the oil over the popcorn, fold over the top of the bag, and shake until the popcorn is coated and moist. Sprinkle the tea leaf mixture over the popcorn, fold over the top of the bag, and shake a few times to coat. Put the popcorn in a large bowl and sprinkle with additional salt if desired.

Smoked Spanish Paprika and Sea Salt Popcorn

This recipe came at the request of a friend who had tried it in a Portland, Oregon, restaurant and loved the combination of the few simple yet highly flavorful ingredients. Unlike Hungarian paprika, Spanish paprika—also called *pimentón de La Vera*—has that warm, smoky element but also an underlying sweetness. There is no heat with this pepper, just treat.

MAKES 4 QUARTS

4 quarts freshly popped corn
2 teaspoons smoked Spanish paprika
2 teaspoons sea salt
2 tablespoons grated Parmesan cheese
3 tablespoons Spanish olive oil

- Put the popcorn in a large, clean paper bag or a washable muslin bag. In a small bowl, combine the paprika, 1 teaspoon of the salt, and Parmesan.

- Drizzle the oil over the popcorn, fold over the top of the bag, and shake until the popcorn is coated and moist. Sprinkle the paprika mixture over the popcorn, fold over the top of the bag, and shake a few times to coat. Transfer to a large bowl and sprinkle the remaining salt over the popcorn.

Pom-Pom Popcorn

The über-trendy pomegranate pairs with hip popcorn in a pleasant, slightly puckery, combination. Look for freeze-dried pomegranate seeds in gourmet grocers or health-food stores. Adjust the amount of pomegranate powder to your liking, and even throw in some extra whole seeds in the end if you wish.

MAKES 4 QUARTS

2 cups freeze-dried pomegranate seeds (arils)
½ teaspoon ground ginger
¼ cup corn oil
¾ cup popcorn kernels
Salt

- In a clean coffee grinder, grind the pomegranate seeds to a powder. Transfer to a small bowl and combine with the ginger.

- In a deep pot, heat the oil over medium heat. Add a few kernels to the pot. Once they pop, add the remaining kernels and shake the pot until they cover the bottom of the pot evenly. Cover the pot and shake intermittently until the popping slows to 5 seconds between pops. Remove the pot from the heat and transfer the popcorn to a large bowl. Season with the salt and sprinkle with the pomegranate mixture, tossing to coat.

Herbes de Provence Popcorn

Sacrebleu! Some fussy French chefs may take exception to flavoring popcorn with this classic Provençal herb mix, but we think it's *magnifique*. The interesting element in this recipe is lavender—see how many folks can guess the secret ingredient. If you don't want to combine the herbs yourself, use two tablespoons of store-bought blend instead. *Bon appétit!*

MAKES 4 QUARTS

4 quarts freshly popped corn
1½ teaspoons dried lavender
1½ teaspoons dried rosemary
½ tablespoon dried thyme
½ tablespoon dried summer savory
2 teaspoons sea salt
¼ cup olive oil

- Put the popcorn in a large, clean paper bag or a washable muslin bag. With a mortar and pestle, crush the lavender and rosemary. In a small bowl, combine the lavender, rosemary, thyme, summer savory, and salt.

- Drizzle the oil over the popcorn, fold over the top of the bag, and shake until the popcorn is coated and moist. Sprinkle the herb mixture over the popcorn, fold over the top of the bag, and shake a few times to coat.

> Popped corn is always white; it is only the hull that is colored.

Parm and Pepper Popcorn

Three pepper flavors—red pepper flakes, black pepper, and paprika (dried and ground sweet red pepper pods)—pair well with nutty-flavored Parmesan cheese and a soupçon of olive oil to create a delicious treat.

MAKES 4 QUARTS

4 quarts freshly popped corn
½ teaspoon red pepper flakes
¼ teaspoon freshly ground black pepper
¼ teaspoon sweet paprika
¼ teaspoon salt
2 tablespoons grated Parmesan cheese
3 tablespoons olive oil

- Put the popcorn in a large, clean paper bag or a washable muslin bag. In a small bowl, combine the red pepper, black pepper, paprika, salt, and Parmesan.

- Drizzle the oil over the popcorn, fold over the top of the bag, and shake until the popcorn is coated and moist. Sprinkle the pepper mixture over the popcorn, fold over the top of the bag, and shake a few times to coat.

Blazin' Cajun Corn

Hooo-wee! Here is one recipe straight from the bayous of Lou-ee-zee-anna that you will love. Fiery flavors cling right onto the popcorn and make you sweat like a sinner in church. But this here is one burn that hurts so good, you'll want to eat the entire bowl yourself. I gaa-ron-tee!

MAKES 4 QUARTS

4 quarts freshly popped corn
⅓ cup butter, melted
2 teaspoons hot smoked paprika
1½ teaspoons onion powder
1½ teaspoons garlic powder
½ teaspoon cayenne pepper
½ teaspoon chili powder
½ teaspoon salt
½ teaspoon lemon pepper

- Preheat the oven to 300°F. Line a baking sheet with foil or a silicone baking sheet and set aside.

- Put the popcorn in a large, clean paper bag or a washable muslin bag. In a small bowl, whisk together the butter, paprika, onion powder, garlic powder, cayenne pepper, chili powder, salt, and lemon pepper. Drizzle the mixture over the popcorn, fold over the top of the bag, and shake until the popcorn is coated and moist.

- Spread the popcorn evenly over the baking sheet and bake until the popcorn is dry, 5 to 7 minutes.

Crabby Corn

There is a distinct flavor associated with crabs and other bivalves along the Chesapeake Bay. A blend of smoldering savory ingredients, it is easily identifiable as a regional specialty. But why should Maryland and Virginia have all the fun? We take that classic favorite seafood seasoning and not much else to create a snack that will leave you feeling delightfully crabby.

MAKES 4 QUARTS

4 quarts freshly popped corn

1 teaspoon freshly squeezed lemon juice

2 tablespoons olive oil

1½ teaspoons seafood seasoning, such as Old Bay

- Put the popcorn in a large, clean paper bag or a washable muslin bag. In a small bowl, whisk together the lemon juice and oil.

- Drizzle the lemon juice mixture over the popcorn, fold over the top of the bag, and shake until the popcorn is coated and moist. Sprinkle the seafood seasoning over the popcorn, fold over the top of the bag, and shake a few times to coat.

Popcorn is on the American Dental Association's list of approved sugar-free snacks.

Classic Barbecue Popcorn

Frito-Lay introduced the barbecue-flavored potato chip in 1965 and changed snack time forever. Here that familiar tang with a little bit of heat and a little bit of sweet makes popcorn a treat so good, we bet you can't eat just one.

MAKES 4 QUARTS

4 quarts freshly popped corn
¼ cup peanut or olive oil
2 tablespoons barbecue sauce
½ teaspoon onion powder
1 teaspoon chili powder
¼ teaspoon ground cumin
½ teaspoon salt
Dash freshly ground black pepper
2 tablespoons grated Parmesan cheese

- Put the popcorn in a large, clean paper bag or a washable muslin bag. In a small bowl, whisk together the oil, barbecue sauce, onion powder, chili powder, cumin, salt, and pepper.

- Drizzle the oil mixture over the popcorn, fold over the top of the bag, and shake until the popcorn is coated and moist. Sprinkle the Parmesan over the popcorn, fold over the top of the bag, and shake a few times to coat.

Chai Spice Popcorn

Rich, exotic chai seasoning comes alive as a coating for popcorn. Warm and full-bodied, there is an undertone of sweetness and an abundance of spice. It's a great accompaniment to watching a good film noir on a rainy weekend.

MAKES 4 QUARTS

4 quarts freshly popped corn
Seeds scraped from one vanilla bean
1½ tablespoons sugar
1 tablespoon black tea leaves, finely ground
1 teaspoon powdered milk
1 teaspoon ground cinnamon
¼ teaspoon ground cloves
¼ teaspoon ground ginger
¼ teaspoon grated nutmeg
Dash freshly ground black pepper
Dash salt
3 tablespoons canola oil

- Put the popcorn in a large, clean paper bag or a washable muslin bag. In a small bowl, stir the vanilla seeds into the sugar. Add the tea leaves, powdered milk, cinnamon, cloves, ginger, nutmeg, pepper, and salt.

- Drizzle the oil over the popcorn, fold over the top of the bag, and shake until the popcorn is coated and moist. Sprinkle the spice mixture over the popcorn, fold over the top of the bag, and shake a few times to coat.

Hot As Heck Popcorn

Some like it hot, and if you are one of them, this liberal coating of fiery mustard powder and pepper will surely fan the flames within. This one's definitely not for folks susceptible to spontaneous combustion.

MAKES 2 QUARTS

1 teaspoon mustard powder
1 teaspoon freshly cracked black pepper
½ teaspoon cayenne pepper
1 teaspoon salt
2 tablespoons corn oil
6 tablespoons popcorn kernels

- In a small bowl, combine the mustard powder, black pepper, cayenne pepper, and salt; set aside.

- Heat the oil in a medium-size pot over medium heat. Add a few kernels to the pot. Once they pop, add the remaining kernels and shake the pot until they cover the bottom of the pot evenly. Cover the pot and shake intermittently as the kernels pop until the popping slows to 5 seconds between pops. Remove the pot from the heat and transfer the popcorn to a large, clean paper bag or a washable muslin bag.

- Immediately sprinkle the spice mixture over the popcorn, fold over the top of the bag, and shake a few times to coat.

Curry Corn

Earthy and ethereal, curry warms the body from the inside out. Making your own curry seasoning is simple, and the flavor easily adapts itself to popcorn for an unforgettable snack. Adding peanuts to the mix can only make something this good even better.

MAKES 4 QUARTS

4 quarts freshly popped corn

1 cup honey-roasted peanuts (optional)

1 teaspoon ground coriander

1 teaspoon ground cumin

1 teaspoon freshly ground black pepper

1 teaspoon turmeric

1 teaspoon ground ginger

1 teaspoon salt

¼ cup peanut oil

- Put the popcorn in a large, clean paper bag or a washable muslin bag. If using the peanuts, add them to the bag. In a small bowl, combine the coriander, cumin, pepper, turmeric, ginger, and salt.

- Drizzle the oil over the popcorn, fold over the top of the bag, and shake until the popcorn is coated and moist. Sprinkle the coriander mixture over the popcorn, fold over the top of the bag, and shake a few times to coat.

General Zuo's Popcorn

General Zuo Zongtang, also known as General Zuo or General Tso, served his country during China's Qing Dynasty. Whatever was his connection to chicken is not known, but there is no doubt it was a saucy one. Spicy, too— much like our homage to the general in this recipe.

4 quarts freshly popped corn

One 13-ounce can dry chow mein noodles

1 cup roasted, salted peanuts

⅓ cup butter, melted

MAKES 4½ QUARTS 1 teaspoon vinegar-based Asian hot sauce, such as Sriracha

1 teaspoon sugar

½ teaspoon garlic powder

2 teaspoons soy sauce

- Preheat the oven to 300°F. Line a baking sheet with foil or a silicone baking sheet and set aside.

- Put the popcorn, noodles, and peanuts in a large, clean paper bag or a washable muslin bag. In a small bowl, whisk together the butter, hot sauce, sugar, and garlic powder. Drizzle the butter mixture over the popcorn, fold over the top of the bag, and shake until the popcorn is coated and moist. Drizzle the soy sauce over the popcorn, fold over the top of the bag, and shake a few times to coat.

- Spread the popcorn evenly over the baking sheet and bake until the popcorn is dry, 5 to 7 minutes.

Spicy Buffalo Popcorn

October 3, 1964, should be honored with a national holiday. It was then that Frank and Teressa Bellisimo, owners of the Anchor Bar in Buffalo, New York, enterprisingly fried up some chicken wings and tossed them in a bath of melted butter and hot sauce. The rest is history. This recipe captures the flavor—and spirit—of that night more than four decades ago. And yes, we suggest you serve this with celery sticks and blue cheese dressing.

MAKES 4 QUARTS

4 quarts freshly popped corn
⅓ cup butter, melted
¼ cup vinegar-based hot sauce, such as Tabasco or Texas Pete
¼ teaspoon freshly ground black pepper
½ teaspoon salt
1 teaspoon sugar
1 teaspoon chili powder

- Preheat the oven to 300°F. Line a baking sheet with foil or a silicone baking sheet and set aside.

- Put the popcorn in a large, clean paper bag or a washable muslin bag. In a medium-size bowl, whisk together the butter, hot sauce, pepper, salt, sugar, and chili powder. Drizzle the mixture over the popcorn, fold over the top of the bag, and shake until the popcorn is coated and moist.

- Spread the popcorn evenly over the baking sheet and bake until the popcorn is dry, 5 to 7 minutes.

Chile-Lime-Tequila Popcorn

The heat of the jalapeño, the coolness of lime, and the *pop!* of tequila come together nicely in this adults-only treat. It's a great snack for munching on the patio with a pitcher of margaritas close at hand—sophisticated, unique, and quite possibly responsible for folks jumping on tables and dancing like Pee-wee Herman. Tequila!

MAKES 4 QUARTS

4 quarts freshly popped corn
⅓ cup butter, melted
2 teaspoons freshly squeezed lime juice
½ teaspoon lime zest
1 teaspoon tequila
½ small jalapeño, seeds and membrane removed, minced
½ teaspoon freshly ground black pepper
1½ teaspoons salt
1 teaspoon red pepper flakes
1 teaspoon ground cumin

- Preheat the oven to 300°F. Line a baking sheet with foil or a silicone baking sheet and set aside.

- Put the popcorn in a large, clean paper bag or a washable muslin bag. In a medium-size bowl, whisk together the butter, lime juice and zest, and tequila. Add the jalapeño. In a small bowl, combine the black pepper, salt, red pepper, and cumin.

- Drizzle the butter mixture over the popcorn, fold over the top of the bag, and shake until the popcorn is coated and moist. Sprinkle the pepper mixture over the popcorn, fold over the top of the bag, and shake a few times to coat.

- Spread the popcorn evenly over the baking sheet and bake until the popcorn is dry, 5 to 7 minutes.

Santa Fe Chipotle Corn

When is a jalapeño not a jalapeño? When it is a chipotle. Chipotles are smoke-dried jalapeños, highly favored in the American West and Mexico. They are often sold in cans, packed in adobe (a flavorful red chile–based sauce). This recipe produces popcorn that is smoky, a bit spicy, and very satisfying. Olé!

MAKES 4 QUARTS

4 quarts freshly popped corn
½ teaspoon chili powder
½ teaspoon ground cinnamon
2 chipotle peppers in adobe sauce
⅓ cup butter, melted

- Preheat the oven to 300°F. Line a baking sheet with foil or a silicone baking sheet and set aside.

- Put the popcorn in a large, clean paper bag or a washable muslin bag. In a small bowl, combine the chili powder and cinnamon. Remove and discard the stems of the peppers, place them on a cutting board, and mash them with the tines of a fork. In a separate bowl, whisk the chipotle mash with the butter until fully incorporated.

- Drizzle the butter mixture over the corn, fold over the top of the bag, and shake until the popcorn is coated and moist. Sprinkle the chili-powder mixture over the popcorn, fold over the top of the bag, and shake a few times to coat.

- Spread the popcorn evenly over the baking sheet and bake until the popcorn is dry, 5 to 7 minutes.

Pesto Popcorn

Pesto is a tasty and versatile amalgamation of classic Italian flavors—olive oil, basil, garlic, Parmesan, and pine nuts. Pasta is often topped with pesto, as is bruschetta. Pesto's rich, nutty flavor works perfectly with popcorn and becomes even more special with the addition of some extra Parmesan and pine nuts.

MAKES 4 QUARTS

4 quarts freshly popped corn
⅓ cup olive oil
1 tablespoon prepared pesto
1 teaspoon dried oregano
1 teaspoon garlic powder
⅓ cup grated Parmesan cheese
½ cup pine nuts, toasted

- Preheat the oven to 300°F. Line a baking sheet with foil or a silicone baking sheet and set aside.

- Put the popcorn in a large, clean paper bag or a washable muslin bag. In a small bowl, whisk together the oil and pesto. Drizzle the oil mixture over the popcorn, fold over the top of the bag, and shake until the popcorn is coated and moist. Sprinkle the oregano and garlic powder over the popcorn, fold over the top of the bag, and shake a few times to coat.

- Spread the popcorn evenly over the baking sheet and bake until the popcorn is dry, 5 to 7 minutes. Transfer to a large bowl, sprinkle the Parmesan over the popcorn, and toss to coat. Sprinkle the pine nuts over the popcorn and toss to combine.

Za'atar Popcorn

Za'atar, a popular seasoning in Lebanon, Israel, and elsewhere in the Middle East, is a mixture of herbs such as oregano, marjoram, thyme, savory, and coriander. Za'atar has been enjoyed since medieval times. Another regional favorite—pistachio nuts—are combined with the popcorn for added flavor and crunch. Enjoy this food in good health, or, as they would say in Lebanon, *suhtain*.

MAKES 4 QUARTS

4 quarts freshly popped corn
1 tablespoon za'atar
¼ teaspoon ground ginger
½ teaspoon salt
¾ cup pistachios, finely chopped
¼ cup olive oil

- Put the popcorn in a large, clean paper bag or a washable muslin bag. In a medium-size bowl, combine the za'atar, ginger, salt, and pistachios.

- Drizzle the oil over the popcorn, fold over the top of the bag, and shake until the popcorn is coated and moist. Sprinkle the pistachio mixture over the popcorn, fold over the top of the bag, and shake a few times to coat.

There are 48 calories in 1 cup of oil-popped popcorn.

Chinese Five-Spice Popcorn

Chinese five-spice powder is a wonderful blend of black pepper, star anise, cinnamon, cloves, and fennel. You can also make your own five-spice blend by combining equal parts of each ingredient.

MAKES 4 QUARTS

4 quarts freshly popped corn

2 tablespoon peanut oil

2 tablespoons soy sauce

1 teaspoon Chinese five-spice powder

½ teaspoon garlic powder

½ teaspoon ground ginger

¼ teaspoon cayenne pepper

¼ teaspoon sugar

⅛ teaspoon salt

2 tablespoons toasted sesame seeds

- Preheat the oven to 300°F. Line a baking sheet with foil or a silicone baking sheet and set aside.

- Put the popcorn in a large, clean paper bag or a washable muslin bag. In a small bowl, whisk together the oil, soy sauce, five-spice powder, garlic powder, ginger, cayenne pepper, sugar, and salt. Drizzle the oil mixture over the popcorn, fold over the top of the bag, and shake until the popcorn is coated and moist.

- Spread the popcorn evenly over the baking sheet and bake until the popcorn is dry, 5 to 7 minutes. Remove the popcorn from the oven, transfer to a large bowl, and sprinkle the sesame seeds over the popcorn.

Black and White Sesame Popcorn

A preponderance of black and white sesame seeds with a little bit of heat from red and black pepper work wonders with popcorn. With a little splash of soy sauce, the taste becomes exotic. The flavor is elusive, but the finished product is delectable.

MAKES 4 QUARTS

4 quarts freshly popped corn
½ teaspoon red pepper flakes
¼ teaspoon freshly ground black pepper
¼ teaspoon ground ginger
¼ teaspoon salt
1 tablespoon white sesame seeds
1 tablespoon black sesame seeds
3 tablespoons canola oil
1 tablespoon soy sauce

- Preheat the oven to 300°F. Line a baking sheet with foil or a silicone baking sheet and set aside.

- Put the popcorn in a large, clean paper bag or a washable muslin bag. In a small bowl, combine the red pepper flakes, black pepper, ginger, salt, ½ tablespoon of the white sesame seeds, and ½ tablespoon of the black sesame seeds. In a separate bowl, whisk together the oil and soy sauce.

- Drizzle the oil mixture over the popcorn, fold over the top of the bag, and shake until the popcorn is coated and moist. Sprinkle the pepper mixture over the popcorn, fold over the top of the bag, and shake a few times to coat.

- Spread the popcorn evenly over the baking sheet and bake until the popcorn is dry, 5 to 7 minutes. Transfer immediately to a large bowl, sprinkle the remaining sesame seeds over the popcorn, and toss to coat.

Wasabi and Ginger Popcorn

This fiery snack gets its heat from two rockin' roots. The first, wasabi (also known as Japanese horseradish), is best known as the ubiquitous green glob beside sushi, and it packs a powerful punch to the taste buds. The second, ginger, is a spice that goes from mild to wild. The two come together here as a wickedly wonderful pair.

MAKES 4 QUARTS

4 quarts freshly popped corn
½ teaspoon salt
½ teaspoon sugar
1 tablespoon black sesame seeds
3 tablespoons butter, melted
2 teaspoons wasabi paste
¼ cup candied ginger, finely chopped
½ cup wasabi-flavored fried peas

- Put the popcorn in a large, clean paper bag or a washable muslin bag. In a small bowl, combine the salt, sugar, and sesame seeds. In a medium-size bowl, whisk together the melted butter and wasabi until fully incorporated; stir in the ginger and peas.

- Drizzle the butter mixture over the popcorn, fold over the top of the bag, and shake until the popcorn is coated and moist. Sprinkle the salt mixture over the popcorn, fold over the top of the bag, and shake a few times to coat.

Yin and Yang Snack Mix

Ah, the ancient Chinese philosophy of yin and yang, the concept that two opposing forces—or, in this case, flavors—can also be complementary. Think of bitter and sweet, or sweet and sour, for some culinary examples. And consider this popcorn recipe, which combines salty and sweet flavors for a deliciously addictive treat.

2 quarts freshly popped corn

½ cup wheat-square cereal, such as Wheat Chex

½ cup miniature pretzels

½ cup dried apple chips, broken

MAKES 3 QUARTS 2 teaspoons onion powder

2 teaspoons garlic powder

½ cup dark or semisweet chocolate chips

½ cup dried cranberries or cherries

¼ cup olive oil

- Put the popcorn, cereal, pretzels, and apple chips in a large, clean paper bag or a washable muslin bag.

- In a small bowl, combine the onion powder and garlic powder. In a medium-size bowl, combine the chocolate chips and cranberries.

- Drizzle the oil over the popcorn mixture, fold over the top of the bag, and shake until the popcorn is coated and moist. Sprinkle the onion-powder mixture over the popcorn, fold over the top of the bag, and shake a few times to coat. Transfer the popcorn mixture to a large bowl, add the chocolate-chip mixture, and stir to combine.

Nacho Nacho Man

This snack has visual appeal and satisfies the appetite. Mixing popcorn with colorful tortilla chips, taco seasoning, jalapeños, and lots of cheddar cheese creates a great party dish that will sate the hunger of your own village people.

MAKES 4 QUARTS

4 quarts freshly popped corn
½ cup regular tortilla chips, broken
½ cup blue-corn tortilla chips, broken
⅓ cup butter, melted
1 tablespoon taco seasoning mix
¼ cup sliced pickled jalapeños from a jar, drained
1 cup sharp cheddar cheese, finely grated

- Preheat the oven to 300°F. Line a baking sheet with foil or a silicone baking sheet and set aside.

- Put the popcorn and chips in a large, clean paper bag or a washable muslin bag. In a small bowl, whisk together the butter and taco seasoning. Drizzle the butter mixture over the popcorn, fold over the top of the bag, and shake until the popcorn is coated and moist.

- Spread the popcorn mixture evenly over the baking sheet and bake until the popcorn is dry, 5 to 7 minutes. Transfer the popcorn mixture to a large baking dish. Sprinkle the jalapeños and cheese over the popcorn. Return to the oven for 2 to 3 minutes, or until the cheese is melted.

Gorgonzola and Green Onion Popcorn

Rich, creamy, and pungent, the complex flavor of gorgonzola cheese teams up with the sharpness of green onions to create a lip-smacking, palate-pleasing snack. Eat out of hand, or use as a topping on baked potatoes or vichyssoise.

MAKES 4 QUARTS

4 quarts freshly popped corn
$\frac{1}{3}$ cup butter, at room temperature
3 ounces gorgonzola cheese, crumbled
2 tablespoons finely chopped green onions
$\frac{1}{4}$ teaspoon freshly ground black pepper
$\frac{1}{4}$ teaspoon salt

- Preheat the oven to 300°F. Line a baking sheet with foil or a silicone baking sheet and set aside.

- Put the popcorn in a large, clean paper bag or a washable muslin bag. In a small microwavable bowl, combine the butter and 2 ounces of the cheese; heat briefly until melted, about 15 seconds. Whisk in 1 tablespoon of the green onions, black pepper, and salt. Drizzle the butter mixture over the corn, fold over the top of the bag, and shake until the popcorn is coated and moist.

- Spread the popcorn evenly over the baking sheet and bake until the popcorn is dry, 5 to 7 minutes. Remove the popcorn from the oven, transfer to a large bowl, and top with the remaining cheese and green onions; toss gently to combine.

Popcorn with Garlic Three Ways

You need not worry about vampires after consuming this garlic-o-rific snack. The mellow, nutty goodness of roasted garlic is combined with the sharpness of raw garlic and the piquant taste of garlic powder. A good helping of parsley and Parmesan cheese round out the mix.

MAKES 4 QUARTS

1 medium head garlic
2 teaspoons olive oil
4 quarts freshly popped corn
⅓ cup butter, melted
2 garlic cloves, minced
1 teaspoon garlic powder
½ teaspoon salt
3 tablespoons grated Parmesan cheese
1 tablespoon finely chopped fresh flatleaf parsley

- Preheat the oven to 350°F.

- With a sharp knife, cut away a small portion—about ¼ inch—from the top of the garlic bulb (the bulb should remain intact but the individual cloves should be visible). Remove as much of the papery skin from the garlic bulb as possible without pulling the bulb apart. Place the bulb in the center of a large square of aluminum foil. Bring the foil up around the bulb, gathering and crimping the foil at the top, but leaving a small opening. Drizzle in the oil. Place the foil-wrapped bulb on a baking sheet and bake for 45 minutes.

- Remove the garlic from the oven and allow to cool for at least 20 to 25 minutes. Meanwhile, reduce the oven temperature to 300°F. Line a baking sheet with foil or a silicone baking sheet and set aside.

- When completely cool, remove the garlic cloves from the bulb and squeeze the contents into a small bowl. Mash the garlic with the tines of a fork until it resembles a smooth paste; set aside.

- Put the popcorn in a large, clean paper bag or a washable muslin bag. In a medium-size bowl, whisk together the butter, garlic paste, minced garlic, garlic powder, and salt. Drizzle the garlic mixture over the popcorn, fold over the top of the bag, and shake until the popcorn is coated and moist.

- Spread the popcorn evenly over the baking sheet and bake until the popcorn is dry, 6 to 8 minutes. Transfer to a large bowl and sprinkle the Parmesan over the popcorn, tossing to coat. Allow to sit about 3 minutes, sprinkle the parsley over the popcorn, and toss to coat.

Pizza Margherita Popcorn

At the cusp of a new century, a pizza maker in Naples, Italy, created a pie to honor a visit to his town by Queen Margherita. The flavor combination from 1899 is still a classic—tomato, cheese, and fresh basil (the colors of which match those of the Italian flag). Although there is no evidence Queen Margherita ever ate popcorn, no doubt if she had sampled this recipe, she would have proclaimed a royal decree in its honor.

MAKES 4 QUARTS

4 quarts freshly popped corn

¼ cup oil-packed sun-dried tomatoes, drained and diced

1 teaspoon dried basil

1 teaspoon dried oregano

½ teaspoon red pepper flakes

½ teaspoon salt

⅓ cup butter, melted

¼ cup grated Parmesan cheese

2 tablespoons fresh basil, chopped

- Preheat the oven to 300°F. Line a baking sheet with foil or a silicone baking sheet and set aside.

- Put the popcorn in a large, clean paper bag or a washable muslin bag. In a small bowl, combine the tomatoes, dried basil, oregano, red pepper flakes, and salt; whisk in the butter. Drizzle the butter mixture over the popcorn, fold over the top of the bag, and shake until the popcorn is coated and moist.

- Spread the popcorn evenly over the baking sheet and bake until the popcorn is dry, 7 to 10 minutes, stirring once. Transfer the popcorn to a large bowl, sprinkle with the Parmesan and fresh basil, and toss to combine.

American Pie Mix

Don McLean had the right idea. Drive your Chevy to the levy and join some good ol' boys in eating popcorn. Maybe they ate this popcorn with crisp apple chips that take on a buttery richness and spice reminiscent of apple pie with its mix of brown sugar, cinnamon, nutmeg, and cloves.

MAKES 4 QUARTS

4 quarts freshly popped corn

2 cups dried apple chips, roughly broken

⅓ cup butter, melted

1 teaspoon ground cinnamon

¼ teaspoon grated nutmeg

⅛ teaspoon ground cloves

2 tablespoons dark brown sugar

¼ teaspoon vanilla extract

½ teaspoon salt

- Preheat the oven to 300°F. Line a baking sheet with foil or a silicone baking sheet and set aside.

- In a large mixing bowl, combine the popcorn and apple chips, tossing to mix. In a small bowl, whisk together the butter, cinnamon, nutmeg, and cloves. Drizzle the butter mixture over the popcorn, stirring well to coat. Sprinkle the brown sugar and vanilla over the popcorn, stirring well to coat.

- Spread the popcorn mixture evenly on a baking sheet and bake until the popcorn is dry, about 10 minutes, stirring once. Transfer to a large bowl, sprinkle the salt over the popcorn, and toss to coat.

Popcorn and Pine-Nut Brittle

Two puffed grains—popcorn and puffed-rice cereal—come together with a little bit of sweet and a little bit of savory that create a sophisticated brittle brimming with flavor. Note: As you dissolve the sugar in the corn syrup, brush only the sides of the pot to remove sugar crystals; it will take the sugar longer to reach the desired temperature if excess water is added to the pot via the brush.

MAKES 8 TO 10
SERVINGS

1½ quarts freshly popped corn

2 cups puffed-rice cereal

1 cup pine nuts, toasted

¾ cup water

1 cup sugar

¼ cup light corn syrup

½ teaspoon freshly squeezed lemon juice

1 tablespoon freshly cracked black pepper

- In a large bowl, combine the popcorn, cereal, and pine nuts, tossing to mix; set aside.

- In a medium-size saucepan, combine the water, sugar, corn syrup, and lemon juice. Cook over medium-high heat, stirring constantly until the sugar dissolves completely and the mixture begins to boil. Keep the sides of the pot clean of sugar crystals by brushing lightly with a minimal amount of water, but only as needed. Cook to a hard-ball stage, or 250°F on a candy thermometer.

- Remove the pan from the heat and stir in the pepper. Pour the syrup over the popcorn mixture, taking care not to burn yourself. With a wooden spoon, toss the popcorn to coat completely.

- Spread the popcorn mixture evenly over a nonstick baking pan. Allow the mixture to cool until hardened; break into pieces and serve.

Popcorn and Seed Brittle

The seed—or kernel—of corn is popped and mixed with other seeds to create a sweet and savory brittle. With so many seeds, you may think this one is for the birds, but after one taste you will want to keep it all to yourself.

4 quarts freshly popped corn
1 cup sunflower seeds, shelled
1 cup pumpkin seeds, toasted
¼ cup sesame seeds, toasted
1 cup light brown sugar

MAKES 20 SERVINGS ½ cup dark corn syrup
½ cup butter
½ teaspoon salt
½ teaspoon baking soda
½ teaspoon cumin
1 teaspoon cinnamon

- Preheat the oven to 250°F. Line a baking sheet with foil or a silicone baking sheet and set aside.

- Put the popcorn in a large bowl. In a medium-size bowl, combine the sunflower seeds, pumpkin seeds, and sesame seeds.

- In a heavy 2-quart saucepan, combine the brown sugar, corn syrup, butter, and salt. Stir constantly over medium heat until the mixture comes to a boil; allow it to boil for 5 minutes without stirring. Remove the pan from the heat; stir in the baking soda, cumin, and cinnamon.

- Pour the mixture over the popcorn, add the seed mixture, and toss to combine. Transfer the popcorn mixture to the baking sheet and bake for 45 minutes, stirring occasionally. Remove the pan from the oven and allow the brittle to cool. Break apart into pieces and serve.

Sweet

No-Kettle Kettle Corn

Ah, the delicious flavor of slightly sweet popcorn, served fresh from huge black cast-iron kettles sitting atop a roaring flame. The sugary aroma wafts above the crowds at county fairs everywhere, calling out like a siren. But what do you do when there's no county fair nearby? And what if you don't have a cast-iron kettle of your own? Simple: Use this recipe and your handy-dandy microwave oven.

MAKES 1 QUART

3 tablespoons popcorn kernels
1 teaspoon canola oil
½ tablespoon sugar
Generous pinch salt

- In a small bowl, combine the kernels and oil; stir to coat. Transfer the kernels to a clean paper lunch bag, fold over the top of the bag ½ inch, and then fold again another ½ inch. Seal the bag with a small strip of cellophane tape.

- Place the bag in the microwave, folded side up, and cook on high for 2 to 3 minutes, or until there are 5 seconds between pops. Open the bag, sprinkle the sugar and salt over the popcorn, and shake a few times to coat.

Popcorn was first mentioned in a cookbook in 1846.

Nice Sugar and Spice Popcorn

This light, simple recipe satisfies a sweet tooth without being sickeningly sweet. A little cinnamon and nutmeg add warmth, making this a great snack to enjoy with a cup of tea or a glass of wine with a little attitude, like a Gewürztraminer.

MAKES 4 QUARTS

4 quarts freshly popped corn
1 vanilla bean
2 teaspoons sugar
1 teaspoon ground cinnamon
¼ teaspoon grated nutmeg
¼ teaspoon salt
1 tablespoon canola oil
¼ teaspoon vanilla extract

- Put the popcorn in a large, clean paper bag or a washable muslin bag. Slice the vanilla bean lengthwise and scrape the seeds from both halves into a small bowl; discard the bean. Stir in the sugar, cinnamon, nutmeg, and salt. In a separate bowl, whisk together the oil and vanilla.

- Drizzle the oil mixture over the popcorn, fold over the top of the bag, and shake until the popcorn is coated and moist. Sprinkle the spice mixture over the popcorn, fold over the top of the bag, and shake a few times to coat.

Cuppa Cappuccino Corn

This caffeinated treat has all the elements of your favorite mug of cappuccino: freshly brewed espresso, milk, sugar, and cinnamon. The only difference is that you crunch it instead of sipping it. Enjoy it while doing *The New York Times* crossword puzzle in a big, comfy chair.

MAKES 4 QUARTS

4 quarts freshly popped corn
2 tablespoons freshly brewed espresso
2 tablespoons sweetened condensed milk
⅓ cup sugar
2 tablespoons butter
¼ teaspoon salt
1 tablespoon powdered creamer
1 teaspoon finely ground espresso-roast coffee
2 teaspoons ground cinnamon

- Preheat the oven to 300°F. Line a baking sheet with foil or a silicone baking sheet and set aside.

- Put the popcorn in a large, clean paper bag or a washable muslin bag. In a medium-size saucepan, heat the espresso, milk, and sugar, whisking constantly until the sugar is fully dissolved. Add the butter and whisk until incorporated. Stir in the salt, creamer, and ground coffee. Bring the coffee mixture to a boil, then remove pan from the heat. Allow the mixture to cool slightly.

- Drizzle the coffee mixture over the popcorn, fold over the top of the bag, and shake until the popcorn is coated and moist. Spread the popcorn evenly over the baking sheet and bake until the popcorn is dry, 6 to 8 minutes. Transfer the popcorn to a large bowl, sprinkle with the cinnamon, and toss to coat.

Mocha Chocalata Latte Corn

Voulez-vous manger avec moi (ce soir)? Before similar words were sung by Patti LaBelle, the invitation came from Tennessee Williams's Blanche DuBois in *A Streetcar Named Desire. Manger* is French for "eat." This sinful, sultry mix of chocolate and coffee would surely meet the approval of Lady Marmalade or Miss DuBois.

MAKES 4 QUARTS

4 quarts freshly popped corn

1 tablespoon hot cocoa mix

1 teaspoon finely ground dark-roast coffee

2 teaspoons plain or hazelnut-flavored powdered creamer

¼ teaspoon salt

⅓ cup butter, melted

2 teaspoons sugar

- Preheat the oven to 300°F. Line a baking sheet with foil or a silicone baking sheet and set aside.

- Put the popcorn in a large, clean paper bag or a washable muslin bag. In a small bowl, combine the cocoa mix, ground coffee, creamer, and salt.

- Drizzle the butter over the popcorn, fold over the top of the bag, and shake until the popcorn is coated and moist. Sprinkle the coffee mixture over the popcorn, fold over the top of the bag, and shake a few times to coat.

- Spread the popcorn evenly over the baking sheet and bake until the popcorn is dry, 7 to 10 minutes. Transfer the popcorn to a large bowl, sprinkle the sugar over the popcorn, and toss to coat.

Maple Morning Popcorn

Mornings in New England: The sun streaks across the sky. Birds chirp outside the window. Maple syrup runs freely from the trees onto piping hot pancakes. No, this isn't a scene in my neighborhood, either. But this popcorn recipe captures that rich, true maple flavor. Eat this as is, use as a topping for ice cream, or enjoy as a breakfast cereal with cold milk poured over the top.

MAKES 4 QUARTS

4 quarts freshly popped corn
$\frac{1}{3}$ cup butter, melted
$1\frac{1}{2}$ tablespoons pure maple syrup
$\frac{1}{2}$ teaspoon vanilla extract
1 teaspoon ground cinnamon
2 tablespoons sugar

- Preheat the oven to 300°F. Line a baking sheet with foil or a silicone baking sheet and set aside.

- Put the popcorn in a large, clean paper bag or a washable muslin bag. In a small bowl, whisk together the butter, maple syrup, vanilla, and cinnamon. Drizzle the butter mixture over the popcorn, fold over the top of the bag, and shake until the popcorn is coated and moist.

- Spread the popcorn evenly over the baking sheet and bake until the popcorn is dry, 5 to 7 minutes. Transfer the popcorn to a large bowl, sprinkle the sugar over the popcorn, and toss to coat.

Popcorn Comfort, Southern Style

When Southerners want hard liquor, it is often bourbon (pronounced *buh-bun*), consumed straight up, on the rocks, mixed with water or a soft drink (pronounced *co-cola*). They'll also bake it into everything from bread pudding to fruit cake. Why, it's only fittin' that we use some to spike popcorn, too.

MAKES 4 QUARTS

4 quarts freshly popped corn
1/3 cup butter, melted
1 tablespoon light corn syrup
2 tablespoons bourbon
1/2 teaspoon vanilla extract
1/2 teaspoon salt
1 cup pecans, chopped
2 tablespoons sugar

- Preheat the oven to 300°F. Line a baking sheet with foil or a silicone baking sheet and set aside.

- Put the popcorn in a large, clean paper bag or a washable muslin bag. In a small bowl, whisk together the butter, corn syrup, bourbon, and vanilla. Drizzle the butter mixture over the popcorn, fold over the top of the bag, and shake until the popcorn is coated and moist. Sprinkle the salt and pecans over the popcorn, fold over the top of the bag, and shake to combine.

- Spread the popcorn mixture evenly over the baking sheet and bake until the popcorn is dry, 5 to 7 minutes. Transfer the popcorn to a large bowl, sprinkle with the sugar, and toss to coat.

Oscar-Night Popcorn

Grace Kelly, Harlow, Jean—picture of a beauty queen. Gene Kelly, Fred Astaire, Ginger Rogers, dance on air. . . . The Golden Age of Hollywood is recaptured in this glitzy popcorn—perfect for munching while watching an old black-and-white movie on the late show or viewing celebs walking the red carpet. This festive treat calls for paste food coloring and edible glitter, which can be found at most cake decorating stores.

¼ cup canola oil

Golden-yellow paste food coloring (optional)

¾ cup popcorn kernels

MAKES 4 QUARTS   3 tablespoons sugar

½ teaspoon salt

Edible gold glitter, as desired

Edible silver glitter, as desired

- Pour the oil in a small bowl. With a toothpick, remove a small drop of food coloring (it is very concentrated; a tiny bit will do the job) and add it to the oil; stir to blend, adding more as needed.

- Pour the colored oil into a deep pot over medium heat. Add a few kernels to the pot. Once they pop, add the remaining kernels and shake the pot until they cover the bottom of the pot evenly. Sprinkle the sugar and salt over the kernels. Cover the pot and shake intermittently until the popping slows to 5 seconds between pops.

- Remove the pot from the heat, hold the lid, and shake the pot a few times. Transfer the popcorn to a large bowl, sprinkle the glitter over the popcorn, and toss to coat.

Loopy Popcorn Rounds

This is a colorful, fruity snack that toucan—I mean, two can—share. Actually, a whole crowd can share. Scrumptious popcorn joins up with marshmallows, cereal loops, and white chocolate. Use a biscuit cutter to make the popcorn rounds, and watch this treat fly off the plate.

MAKES 18 ROUNDS

4 quarts freshly popped corn

6 tablespoons butter

5 cups miniature marshmallows

1 cup fruit-flavored loop-shaped cereal, such as
   Fruit Loops

1 cup white chocolate chips

• Butter a 9- by 13-inch pan; set aside. Put the popcorn in a large mixing bowl. Melt the butter in a large saucepan over low heat. Add the marshmallows and cook until melted, stirring constantly. Pour the marshmallow mixture over the popcorn and, working quickly, stir gently with a wooden spoon until the popcorn is coated. Stir in the cereal and chocolate chips.

• Transfer the popcorn mixture to the prepared pan. With buttered hands, press the mixture evenly into the pan and allow to cool completely. Using a biscuit cutter, punch circles out of the mixture and serve.

> Seventy percent of all popcorn consumed in America is eaten at home.

S'more Popcorn, Please!

A favorite from childhood, s'mores are a time-honored culinary tradition—the lip-smacking combination of marshmallows, graham crackers, and chocolate. Why not throw popcorn into the mix? These bars of sweet goodness will definitely have folks asking for s'more.

MAKES 24 SQUARES

4 quarts freshly popped corn
6 tablespoons butter
5 cups miniature marshmallows
1 cup honey graham cracker cereal
1½ cups milk chocolate chips

- Butter a 9- by 13-inch pan; set aside. Put the popcorn in a large mixing bowl. In a large saucepan, melt the butter over low heat. Add the marshmallows and cook until melted, stirring constantly. Pour the marshmallow mixture over the popcorn and, working quickly, stir gently with a wooden spoon until the popcorn is coated. Stir in the cereal and 1 cup of the chocolate chips.

- Transfer the popcorn mixture to the prepared pan. With buttered hands, press the mixture evenly into the pan; allow to cool slightly. Melt the remaining chocolate chips according to package instructions and drizzle the chocolate over the popcorn mixture. Allow to cool completely, 20 to 25 minutes, then cut into squares.

Silly Sushi Treats

What makes this sushi so silly—and delicious—is that it isn't really sushi at all, but rather a tasty dessert rendition of the Japanese classic. With a popcorn platform, we top each "roll" with a candy fish and wrap it with a (faux) nori strip made from a piece of fruit leather.

MAKES 24 PIECES

2 quarts freshly popped corn

3 tablespoons butter

1½ teaspoons vanilla-flavored instant pudding mix

2½ cups miniature marshmallows

24 fish-shaped gummy candies, such as Swedish Fish

3 pieces of fruit leather

- Butter a 9- by 13-inch pan; set aside. Put the popcorn in a large mixing bowl. Melt the butter in a large saucepan over low heat. Stir in the pudding mix until dissolved. Add the marshmallows and cook until melted, stirring constantly. Pour the marshmallow mixture over the popcorn and, working quickly, stir gently with a wooden spoon until the popcorn is coated.

- Transfer the popcorn mixture to the prepared pan. With buttered hands, press the mixture evenly into the pan and allow to cool completely. Cut into 12 rectangles slightly larger than a piece of fish candy. Slice each rectangle in half lengthwise and place a candy atop each rectangle.

- To make the "nori," roll out the fruit leather and cut into thin strips about 2 inches long. Wrap a fruit leather strip around the center of each piece of "sushi" to hold the candy in place.

PBP&J Sandwiches

The classic sandwich combination—peanut butter and jelly—pops to new heights with the addition of popcorn. Tasty triangles stuffed with a favorite jam or jelly become decadently delicious when you add peanut butter, marshmallows, and graham cracker cereal to the mix. Perfect for kids' parties and lunch boxes.

MAKES 48
HALF-SANDWICHES

4 quarts freshly popped corn
6 tablespoons butter
½ cup creamy peanut butter
5 cups miniature marshmallows
1 cup honey graham cracker cereal
Jam or jelly

- Butter a 9- by 13-inch pan; set aside. Put the popcorn in a large mixing bowl. Melt the butter and peanut butter in a large saucepan over low heat. Stir in the marshmallows and cook until melted, stirring constantly. Pour the marshmallow mixture over the popcorn and, working quickly, stir gently with a wooden spoon until the popcorn is coated. Stir in the cereal.

- Transfer the popcorn mixture to the prepared pan. With buttered hands, press the mixture evenly into the pan and allow to cool completely. Cut into 24 generous squares; cut each square in half. Spread the jam over one half; top with other half. Cut each "sandwich" diagonally and pierce with a toothpick for serving.

Hawaiian Luau Bars

Sweet fragrances from a multitude of exotic flowers and tropical fruits drift on the trade winds through the Hawaiian islands, perfuming the state with their richness. The ambience is captured in this treat with citrus zest, coconut, macadamia nuts, and pineapple. Cook 'em, Danno.

4 quarts freshly popped corn

One 12-ounce bag white chocolate chips

1 teaspoon lemon zest

MAKES 24 SERVINGS 1 teaspoon orange zest

1 tablespoon sweetened coconut flakes

¼ cup macadamia nuts, chopped

¼ cup candied pineapple, chopped

• Spread the popcorn evenly but compactly on a baking sheet lined with waxed paper or a silicone baking sheet. Melt the chocolate chips according to package instructions. Immediately stir in the lemon zest, orange zest, coconut, macadamia nuts, and pineapple. Pour the chocolate mixture over the popcorn, spreading gently with a wooden spoon. Allow the chocolate mixture to harden, 20 to 25 minutes, then break into pieces and serve.

Americans eat about 17 billion quarts of popcorn each year.

Popcorn-Nut Munch

Elk. Deer. Moose. Caribou. What these four-legged mammals have to do with popcorn, nuts, and chocolate is a mystery, but at least one of the animals is closely linked with a snack mix combining those ingredients. In fairness to the other antlered creatures, we've come up with our own version.

MAKES 20 SERVINGS

4 quarts freshly popped corn
¼ cup pecan halves
¼ cup walnut halves
¼ cup hazelnuts
¼ cup macadamia nuts
1 cup dark brown sugar
½ cup dark corn syrup
½ cup butter
½ teaspoon salt
½ teaspoon baking soda
1 teaspoon vanilla extract
2 cups milk chocolate chips

- Preheat the oven to 250°F. Line a baking sheet with foil or a silicone baking sheet and set aside.

- Put the popcorn in a large bowl. In a medium-size bowl, combine the pecans, walnuts, hazelnuts, and macadamia nuts.

- Place a heavy 2-quart saucepan over medium heat, and add the brown sugar, corn syrup, butter, and salt. Stir constantly until the mixture reaches a boil, then allow it to boil for 5 minutes without stirring. Remove the pan from the heat and stir in the baking soda and vanilla.

- Pour the sugar mixture over the popcorn, add the nut mixture, and toss to combine. Spread the popcorn mixture evenly over the baking sheet and bake for 45 minutes, stirring occasionally.

- Remove the baking sheet from the oven and allow the popcorn to cool. Break the mixture into medium-size pieces.

- Melt the chocolate chips according to package instructions. Line another baking sheet with foil or a silicone baking sheet. Dip each piece of the popcorn mixture into the chocolate to coat on all sides. Place the pieces on the baking sheet and allow the chocolate to harden, about 15 minutes.

Bear Snack

Perfect for a teddy bear tea party or anytime little fingers want a snack, this mix combines popcorn with sugar, honey, spices, and, for added fun, bear-shaped gummy candies and graham crackers.

MAKES 4 QUARTS

4 quarts freshly popped corn

2 teaspoons sugar

1 teaspoon ground cinnamon

¼ teaspoon grated nutmeg

¼ teaspoon salt

3 tablespoons canola oil

1 tablespoon honey

¼ teaspoon vanilla extract

1 cup bear-shaped gummy candies

1 cup bear-shaped graham crackers

- Preheat the oven to 300°F. Line a baking sheet with foil or a silicone baking sheet and set aside.

- Put the popcorn in a large, clean paper bag or a washable muslin bag. In a small bowl, combine the sugar, cinnamon, nutmeg, and salt. In a separate bowl, whisk together the oil, honey, and vanilla.

- Drizzle the oil mixture over the popcorn, fold over the top of the bag, and shake until the popcorn is coated and moist. Sprinkle the sugar mixture over the popcorn, fold over the top of the bag, and shake a few times to coat.

- Spread the popcorn evenly over the baking sheet and bake until the popcorn is dry, 5 to 7 minutes. Transfer the popcorn to a large bowl, add the candies and graham crackers, and toss to combine.

Nut 'n' Honey Mix

Sweet, sticky popcorn and salty peanuts are a perfect match. The combination of the honey and the nuts is, well, just fabulous. Nut'n left to say!

MAKES 4 QUARTS

4 quarts freshly popped corn
1/3 cup butter, melted
1 tablespoon honey
1/4 teaspoon vanilla extract
3/4 cups honey-roasted peanuts, coarsely chopped
1/4 teaspoon salt
2 tablespoons sugar

- Preheat the oven to 300°F. Line a baking sheet with foil or a silicone baking sheet and set aside.

- Put the popcorn in a large, clean paper bag or a washable muslin bag. In a small bowl, whisk together the butter, honey, and vanilla. Drizzle the butter mixture over the popcorn, fold over the top of the bag, and shake until the popcorn is coated and moist. Add the peanuts and salt, fold over the top of the bag, and shake a few times to coat.

- Spread the popcorn evenly over the baking sheet and bake until the popcorn is dry, 7 to 10 minutes. Remove the baking sheet from the oven and immediately sprinkle the sugar evenly over the popcorn; stir gently to coat.

Approximately 1,600 popcorn kernels fill a 1-cup measurement.

Popcorn Colada Balls

The flavors of piña coladas—pineapple and coconut with a cherry on top—join up in these tropical-themed popcorn balls. Be aware: Working with gelatin can be messy, and you have to work quickly, so an extra pair of hands to assist with preparation and cleanup may be in order, but these babies are worth the trouble.

MAKES 18
POPCORN BALLS

4 quarts freshly popped corn
1 cup sugar
1 cup light corn syrup
3 ounces pineapple-flavored gelatin mix
½ cup dried cherries
½ cup sweetened coconut flakes

- Put the popcorn in a large bowl. Line a baking sheet with waxed paper or a silicone baking sheet and set aside. Combine the sugar, corn syrup, and gelatin in a medium-size saucepan and bring to a boil, stirring occasionally.

- Remove the pan from the heat and pour the gelatin mixture over the popcorn; stir gently with a wooden spoon to coat. Quickly add the cherries and coconut and stir to incorporate. With buttered hands, shape the popcorn mixture into tennis ball–size servings. Transfer to the baking sheet and allow to cool.

Death by Chocolate Popcorn Balls

If you have to go, you might as well go with rich, decadent chocolate lingering on your tongue. So says my friend, Marcel Desaulniers, owner of The Trellis restaurant in Williamsburg, Virginia, and creator of the famous—or is it infamous?—Death by Chocolate dessert. Marcel was kind enough to provide me with a favorite recipe of his for chocolate ganache, so we combine it with popcorn for a chocolaty treat to, well, die for. Note: This is definitely a two-person job, so ask a friend to share the fun.

4 quarts freshly popped corn

1 cup heavy cream

¼ cup plus 2 tablespoons unsalted butter

1 cup plus 2 tablespoons sugar

6 ounces semisweet chocolate, chopped into
   ¼-inch pieces

**MAKES 18
POPCORN BALLS**

3 ounces unsweetened chocolate, chopped into
   ¼-inch pieces

2 ounces white chocolate, chopped into ¼-inch pieces

½ cup light corn syrup

½ teaspoon salt

1 teaspoon vanilla extract

½ teaspoon baking soda

½ cup cocoa powder

1½ cups semisweet chocolate chips

- Put the popcorn in a large bowl. Line a baking sheet with waxed paper or a silicone baking sheet and set aside.

- Prepare the ganache by heating the cream, 2 tablespoons of the butter, and 2 tablespoons of the sugar in a medium-size saucepan over medium-high heat, stirring until the sugar has fully dissolved. Bring to a boil. Place the chocolate pieces in a large stainless-steel bowl. Pour the cream mixture over the chocolate and allow to stand for 5 minutes. Stir until fully combined and smooth. Allow the ganache to cool to room temperature, 20 to 25 minutes.

- In a large saucepan, combine the remaining butter, remaining sugar, corn syrup, and salt over medium heat and bring to a boil, stirring constantly. Boil for 2 minutes, continuing to stir. Remove the pan from the heat and stir in the vanilla, baking soda, and 3 tablespoons of the cocoa powder with a wooden spoon.

- Pour the sugar mixture over the popcorn, add the chocolate chips, and stir until the popcorn is coated. With buttered hands, quickly form the popcorn mixture into tennis ball–size servings and hand to a helper. Have the helper make a well in the center of each ball with his/her thumb and quickly spoon in the ganache to fill the well halfway. Mold the popcorn to cover the hole and enclose the ganache. Roll each ball in the remaining cocoa powder and allow to cool on the baking sheet.

Chocolate–Peanut Butter Popcorn Balls

Do you like peanut butter cups? You'll love these chocolate popcorn balls with a delicious dollop of peanut butter filling—perfect for chocoholics and peanut butter freaks alike.

MAKES 34
POPCORN BALLS

4 quarts freshly popped corn

1 cup granulated sugar

1 cup light corn syrup

3 ounces chocolate or chocolate fudge instant pudding mix

½ cup butter, at room temperature

1 cup creamy peanut butter

2 cups confectioners' sugar

1 teaspoon vanilla extract

¼ cup heavy cream

- Put the popcorn in a large bowl. Line a baking sheet with waxed paper or a silicone baking sheet and set aside.

- Combine the granulated sugar, corn syrup, and pudding mix in a medium-size saucepan and bring to a boil, stirring occasionally. Remove the pan from heat and pour the sugar mixture over the popcorn. Stir with a wooden spoon until the popcorn is coated. With buttered hands, shape the popcorn into golf ball–size servings, place on the baking sheet, and use your thumb to make an indentation in the center of each ball. Allow to cool on the baking sheet.

- To make the peanut butter filling, in a medium-size bowl, cream the butter and peanut butter together. Add one third of the confectioners' sugar and mix well to incorporate. Add the vanilla and half of the cream; blend thoroughly. Add another third of the confectioners' sugar and mix well. Add the remaining cream and blend thoroughly. Slowly add the remaining confectioners' sugar until the desired consistency is reached. If the filling is too loose, add more sugar; if it is too hard, add more cream.
- Spoon about 1 tablespoon of the peanut butter filling into each popcorn ball indentation and serve.

Bananas Foster Mix

The taste of the Big Easy meets popcorn in this addictive recipe. Brown sugar, rum, and banana combined with popcorn creates a sweet, crunchy snack. Eat out of hand, use to top a dish of vanilla ice cream, or fold a handful into a crepe with some fresh whipped cream.

MAKES 2 QUARTS

2 quarts freshly popped corn
½ cup butter
1 cup brown sugar
1 teaspoon vanilla extract
1 teaspoon banana extract
2 tablespoons dark rum
1 cup dried banana chips

- Preheat the oven to 300°F. Line a baking sheet with foil or a silicone baking sheet and set aside.

- Put the popcorn in a large bowl. In a small saucepan, melt the butter. Add the brown sugar and whisk constantly until smooth, about 5 minutes. Add the vanilla, banana extract, and rum; whisk until fully incorporated. Remove the pan from the heat and immediately pour the mixture over the popcorn. Stir with a wooden spoon until the popcorn is coated and moist.

- Spread the popcorn evenly over the baking sheet and bake until the popcorn is dry, 5 to 7 minutes. Transfer the popcorn to a large bowl. Add the banana chips and toss to combine.

Candy Cane Corn

Three simple ingredients: one tasty holiday treat. Delight your taste buds any time of the year with crunchy popcorn clusters, smooth white chocolate, and zesty peppermint.

MAKES 24 SERVINGS

4 quarts freshly popped corn
1 bag white chocolate chips
⅔ cup finely crushed candy canes

• Put the popcorn in a large mixing bowl. Line a baking sheet with foil or a silicone baking sheet and set aside. Melt the chocolate chips according to package instructions.

• Drizzle the chocolate over the popcorn, gently stirring with a wooden spoon to incorporate. Spread the popcorn evenly over the baking sheet and immediately sprinkle the crushed candy canes over the popcorn, lightly pressing the candy down with a wooden spoon. Allow the chocolate to cool and harden, then break into pieces and serve.

And More

Chesapeake Bay Crab Cakes

Throughout the delicate estuary of the Chesapeake Bay, the blue crab holds court with an iron claw. Blues are favorites in Virginia, Maryland, and beyond, and they're often served up as crab cakes. This version is adapted from a recipe by my friend John Shields, owner of Gertrude's restaurant in Baltimore, author of several coastal cooking–themed cookbooks, and host of two cookbook-companion television series on PBS.

MAKES 4 SERVINGS

1 egg

2 tablespoons mayonnaise

1 teaspoon dry mustard

½ teaspoon ground black pepper

1 teaspoon seafood seasoning, such as Old Bay

2 teaspoons Worcestershire sauce

Dash of hot sauce

1 pound lump or backfin crabmeat, picked over for shells

½ cup cracker crumbs

½ cup coarsely chopped popcorn crumbs

- In a blender or medium-size mixing bowl, combine the egg, mayonnaise, mustard, pepper, seafood seasoning, Worcestershire, and hot sauce. Mix until frothy. Place the crabmeat in a separate bowl; sprinkle the cracker and popcorn crumbs over the crabmeat. Pour the egg mixture over the crabmeat and gently toss to combine, taking care not to break up the crabmeat.

- Form the crab cakes, by hand or with an ice cream scoop, into 4 rounded mounds about 3 inches in diameter and 1 inch thick. The crab cakes should be as loose as possible yet still hold their shape—don't pack the mixture too firmly. The cakes may be sautéed (in oil or a combination of oil and butter—enough to coat the pan), broiled, or deep fried in oil heated to 375°F. If deep fried, allow the crab cakes to drain on paper towels. Cooking time is brief—about 3 minutes on each side, or until the cakes are golden brown.

Jalapeño "Pop"pers

Like a Chihuahua, the jalapeño pepper is compact but can deliver a big bite—at least on the ankles. Tame the Chihuahua within the fruit (yes, a jalapeño is a fruit) by removing the seeds and membranes, which are carriers of eye-watering capsicum. Now what? Stuff 'em, bake 'em, and, well, you can figure out the rest of the hair-of-the-dog analogy.

MAKES 4 TO 5
SERVINGS

¼ cup coarsely chopped popcorn crumbs
4 slices of bacon, finely chopped
¼ cup diced onions
8 ounces cream cheese, at room temperature
¼ cup shredded sharp cheddar cheese
¼ cup shredded jack cheese
12 to 18 fresh jalapeño peppers

- Preheat the oven to 350°F. Line a baking sheet with foil or a silicone baking sheet and set aside.

- Put the popcorn crumbs in a large bowl. In a medium-size skillet, fry the bacon and onions until the bacon is crisp and the onions are translucent. Remove from the heat, drain, and pour over the popcorn crumbs, stirring to combine. In a medium-size bowl, stir together the cheeses to combine. Fold the cheeses into the popcorn mixture.

- Place 12 to 18 toothpicks (as many as you have jalapeños) in a small bowl filled with enough water to cover them; let them soak for about 1 hour. Cut the caps off the jalapeños and reserve. Scrape out and discard the seeds and membranes. Stuff the jalapeños with the popcorn mixture, replace the jalapeño caps, and hold in place with the damp toothpicks. Place the jalapeños on the baking sheet, and bake until the peppers are tender and heated through, 25 to 35 minutes.

Salchipapa Popcorn

A friend of mine from Colombia told me about this ever-present street food in his country. The basic elements are hot dog–style sausages, potatoes, and some creative mix-ins. Popcorn is commonly used, he says, because it is tasty and filling and adds bulk to stretch the snack for those on a budget.

MAKES 5 QUARTS

1 pound fingerling potatoes, scrubbed clean

⅓ cup salt

¼ cup plus 2 tablespoons olive oil

1 pound Spanish or Portuguese chorizo sausage, sliced on the bias ¼-inch thick

1 teaspoon minced garlic

¼ cup white onion, minced

¼ cup green bell pepper, minced

4 quarts freshly popped corn

1 teaspoon garlic powder

1 teaspoon freshly ground black pepper

1 teaspoon red pepper flakes

1 teaspoon ground coriander

1 cup plantain chips

2 cups fried pork rinds

¼ cup cilantro, roughly chopped

- Put the potatoes in a large pot filled with 1 quart of water. Add the salt and bring to a boil. Cook until the potatoes are fork-tender, 15 to 20 minutes; drain and transfer to a cooling rack. Once cooled, cut the potatoes into thick slices on the bias.

- Preheat the oven to 300°F. Line a baking sheet with foil or a silicone baking sheet and set aside.

- Heat 2 tablespoons of the oil in a heavy pot; add the sausage and sauté for 1 to 2 minutes. Add the minced garlic, onion, and bell pepper; cook until the onions are translucent and the sausage is lightly browned. Remove with a slotted spoon to a plate lined with paper towels. Reserve the oil in the pot.

- Fry the potatoes in the reserved oil until browned, 7 to 10 minutes. Remove with a slotted spoon to the plate with the sausage.

- Put the popcorn in a large, clean paper bag or a washable muslin bag. In a medium-size bowl, combine the garlic powder, black pepper, red pepper flakes, and coriander. Drizzle the remaining oil over the popcorn, fold over the top of the bag, and shake until the popcorn is coated and moist. Sprinkle the garlic-pepper mixture over the popcorn, fold over the top of the bag, and shake a few times to coat.

- Spread the popcorn evenly over the baking sheet and bake until the popcorn is dry, 5 to 7 minutes. Transfer to a large bowl. Add the sausage and potatoes; toss well to combine. Add the plantain chips, pork rinds, and cilantro; toss well to combine.

The best location to store popcorn
is in a cool, dry place.

Poppin' Codfish

Once you've tried this recipe, you'll never think of fish 'n' chips in the same way again. Popcorn's texture gives cod fillets a pleasing crunch, complementing the obligatory french fries. Serve wrapped in yesterday's newspaper for that authentic touch.

Four 6-ounce cod fillets

Salt

Freshly ground black pepper

MAKES 4 SERVINGS Seafood seasoning, such as Old Bay

½ cup all-purpose flour

1 cup thin tempura batter

2 quarts freshly popped corn, slightly crushed

- Fill a deep fat fryer with oil according to manufacturer's instructions and preheat to 350°F. (You can also fry the fish in a deep skillet with enough oil added to cover the fillets. Take care with the hot oil and use a splatter guard.) Cut each cod fillet into three 2-ounce strips and season with salt, pepper, and seafood seasoning. Toss the strips in the flour, dip each strip in the tempura batter, and roll in the popcorn. Add each strip to the fryer; fry the cod until golden brown, 3 to 5 minutes. Drain on paper towels, then serve.

One cup of popcorn has as much fiber as ½ cup of bran flakes.

"Pop!" Goes the Scallop

Scallops are wonderful—their tender, sweet flesh is great backdrop for bold flavors. Here we take plump, meaty scallops, sear them, and brush them with a sweet and savory honey-soy sauce. The sauce not only flavors the scallops, it is the perfect adherent for the popcorn crumbs, which add a delightful crunch to the finished dish.

MAKES 2 TO 3
SERVINGS

1 cup freshly popped corn, at room temperature

2 tablespoons soy sauce

3 tablespoons honey

Dash garlic powder

Freshly ground black pepper

1 dozen U-10 scallops, muscles removed

Salt

Corn oil

- Preheat the oven to 400°F.

- Coarsely chop the popcorn in a food processor and set aside. In a small bowl, whisk together the soy sauce, honey, garlic powder, and a dash of pepper.

- Season the scallops to taste with salt and pepper on both sides. Pour enough oil in a 12-inch sauté pan to just cover the bottom. Heat the pan over medium heat to the smoke point. Add the scallops to the pan briefly, turning once, to sear both sides, cooking for 20 to 30 seconds on each side. (The scallops are done when they transition from translucent to opaque.)

- Place the scallops on a wire rack on top of a baking sheet. Brush each scallop with the honey-soy mixture and sprinkle the popcorn crumbs over the scallops, pressing them into the scallops with the back of a spoon to help the crumbs stick. Bake until the popcorn crumbs are slightly golden, about 2 minutes. Remove the scallops from the oven and transfer to a serving platter.

Popcorn Shrimp

Truth in advertising: This version of popcorn shrimp really includes popcorn. Dredged in popcorn crumbs, flour, and seasonings, these are definitely shrimp you will want to pop in your mouth.

MAKES 2 TO 3 SERVINGS

1 cup freshly popped corn, at room temperature

24 large shrimp, peeled and deveined

Salt and freshly ground black pepper

Seafood seasoning, such as Old Bay

½ teaspoon lemon zest

½ cup all-purpose flour

2 eggs, beaten

Corn oil

- Coarsely chop the popcorn in a food processor and set aside. Season the shrimp with salt, pepper, seafood seasoning, and lemon zest. Holding each shrimp by the tail, dredge with flour, shaking off the excess. Dip in the eggs, then dredge in the popcorn crumbs. Place the coated shrimp on a plate until all are prepared.

- Pour enough oil in a 12-inch sauté pan to cover the bottom with ¼ inch of oil. Heat the pan over medium heat just to the smoke point. The oil should be hot enough to fry the shrimp but not burn. Add the shrimp to the sauté pan and cook until the flesh is firm and pink in color, about 2 minutes on each side. Remove from the pan with a slotted spoon and drain on a paper towel. Serve.

Pacific Rim Pork Chops

Delicious flavors of the Pacific Rim accent these pork chops, which have an element of crunch from the popcorn topping. The chops get their Asian flavor and lacquer sheen from the teriyaki sauce; *teri* refers to shine or luster, and *yaki* describes the grilling method used.

MAKES 4 SERVINGS

Corn oil

Four 8-ounce bone-in pork loin chops

Salt and freshly ground black pepper

$\frac{1}{4}$ teaspoon ground cinnamon

1 teaspoon mustard seeds

$\frac{1}{2}$ cup teriyaki sauce

$\frac{1}{4}$ cup green onions cut into thin rings

$1\frac{1}{2}$ quarts freshly popped corn, slightly crushed

- Preheat the oven to 425°F.
- Add enough oil to coat the bottom of a 10-inch sauté pan. Heat over medium heat to the smoking point.
- Season the pork chops with salt, pepper, cinnamon, and mustard seeds, rubbing the seasonings into the meat. Pan-sear both sides of the pork chops, 20 to 30 seconds on each side.
- Brush the pork chops with the teriyaki sauce and place them on a wire rack in a baking pan. Roast to an internal temperature of 150°F, about 20 minutes. Flip the pork chops halfway through roasting and brush with teriyaki sauce at least twice. Remove from the oven and brush the pork chops a final time with teriyaki sauce. Sprinkle the green onions and popcorn over the pork chops. Place the baking pan back in the oven until the popcorn begins to brown slightly, about 2 minutes. Remove from the oven and serve.

Mac and Cheese Gratin

What happens when you combine two classic comfort foods? No—not pizza topped with mashed potatoes! Check this out: a big serving of hot, creamy macaroni and cheese with a crunchy popcorn topping. Mmm, good.

MAKES 6 SERVINGS

8 ounces elbow macaroni

8 ounces sharp cheddar cheese, shredded

12 ounces small-curd cottage cheese

8 ounces sour cream

½ cup milk

1 teaspoon dry mustard

½ teaspoon salt

¼ teaspoon freshly ground black pepper

¼ teaspoon cayenne pepper

4 cups freshly popped corn

⅓ cup butter, melted

½ teaspoon dried parsley flakes

- Preheat the oven to 350°F.

- Cook and drain the macaroni according to package instructions until al dente. Meanwhile, in a large bowl, combine the cheeses, sour cream, milk, mustard, salt, black pepper, and cayenne pepper; stir well. Pour the drained hot macaroni into the cheese mixture and stir until well blended. Transfer the macaroni mixture to a 9- by 13-inch baking dish.

- Put the popcorn in a large bowl and crush it slightly with the back of a wooden spoon. Drizzle the butter over the popcorn and toss to coat. Sprinkle the parsley over the popcorn and toss to coat.

- Sprinkle the popcorn topping over the pasta mixture and bake 30 to 35 minutes, or until the top is golden brown.

"Pop"corn Bread

A little play on words and a whole lot of flavor, this take on traditional corn bread makes good use of its signature ingredient by adding another level of tasty texture. Be aware that some of the popcorn will sink into the mixture at the start of baking. Add more popcorn for presentation, if desired.

MAKES 16 SERVINGS

4 eggs
One 14.5-ounce can yellow corn, drained
One 14.5-ounce can creamed corn
16 ounces sour cream
16 ounces corn muffin mix
1 teaspoon salt
1 teaspoon pepper
½ pound (2 sticks) butter, melted
1½ quarts freshly popped corn

- Preheat the oven to 325°F.

- In a blender or large mixer bowl, beat the eggs for 2 minutes on medium speed. Add all the canned corns and sour cream; mix on low speed until incorporated. Add the muffin mix, salt, and pepper; mix on low speed until the mixture is smooth. Slowly add the butter and continue mixing for 1 minute, or until the mixture is fully blended.

- Coat an 8-inch-square baking dish with nonstick cooking spray. Add the corn-bread batter and spread evenly in the pan. Top with enough popcorn to cover the surface of the batter. Bake for 50 minutes.

- Raise the oven temperature to 350°F and bake for an additional 5 minutes. The corn bread is done when the edges are golden brown and when a cake tester or toothpick inserted in the center comes out clean. Remove the dish from the oven and allow the corn bread to cool slightly before cutting into 16 squares.

Stuffed Baked Apples à la Mode

Baked apples are kind of like apple pie but with the crust on the inside of the cored fruit. This recipe brings together walnuts, dried fruit, and maple syrup with popcorn crumbs for a tasty filling. The type of apple you pick is up to you. Any of the following baking apples are great: Winesap, Braeburn, Fuji, Pink Lady, Rome Beauty, or Empire.

MAKES 6 SERVINGS

1 cup freshly popped corn, at room temperature
2 ounces (¼ cup) walnuts, coarsely chopped
1 tablespoon golden raisins
1 tablespoon dried cranberries
1 tablespoon dried cherries
½ teaspoon ground cinnamon
¼ teaspoon salt
¾ cup pure maple syrup
6 medium baking apples
Freshly squeezed lemon juice
6 tablespoons butter
Vanilla ice cream

- Preheat the oven to 350°F. Butter a 1½-quart baking dish and set aside.

- Coarsely chop the popcorn in a food processor and set aside. In a medium-size bowl, combine the popcorn crumbs, walnuts, raisins, cranberries, cherries, cinnamon, and salt. Drizzle in enough maple syrup to bind the mixture.

- Core the apples and remove the peel from the top two thirds of each apple. Brush the lemon juice on the peeled part of the apples to prevent browning. Place the apples in the prepared baking dish. Stuff the popcorn mixture into the center of each apple, allowing some to spill out over the top. Drizzle each apple with about 1 teaspoon of maple syrup.

- In a medium-size saucepan over low heat, combine the remaining maple syrup and butter, stirring until fully incorporated. Bake the apples, uncovered, for 30 to 35 minutes or until fork-tender. Transfer the apples to dessert plates and drizzle equal amounts of the maple-butter and a sprinkling of any remaining popcorn mixture on and around the plate. Top each apple with a large scoop of ice cream.

Some of the first popcorn "poppers" were made from fired clay set near an open fire.

A Cracker Jack of a Cake

The fantastic flavors of chocolate, caramel, peanuts, and—of course—popcorn meld in this layer cake. Cool and refreshing, it is great for backyard cookouts, picnics, or ball games.

MAKES 8 SERVINGS

One 18.25-ounce box chocolate cake mix
1½ cups whipping cream
¼ cup sugar
½ teaspoon vanilla extract
½ cup toffee pieces
¾ cup caramel sauce
1½ quarts freshly popped corn, lightly salted
½ cup honey-roasted peanuts
½ cup semisweet chocolate, melted

- Prepare the cake mix according to package directions. Divide the batter evenly between two 9-inch-square pans coated with nonstick cooking spray. Bake according to package directions. Allow the cake layers to cool to room temperature.

- In a large bowl, whip the cream with the sugar and vanilla until the mixture forms medium-stiff peaks. Place the bowl in the refrigerator to keep chilled.

- Remove the cakes from their pans. Trim rounded tops from the layers to make the cakes even in thickness. Place one cake layer on a plate and top with enough whipped cream to form an even ½-inch layer. Sprinkle the toffee over the whipped cream. Place the second layer on top.

- Use the remaining whipped cream to coat the entire cake, using an offset spatula to make the top and sides straight and smooth. Place the cake in the freezer for at least 30 minutes.

- Pour the caramel sauce over the center of the cake. Spread the sauce evenly with a spatula, allowing some of the caramel to run over the sides. Place the cake back in the freezer for an additional 5 minutes, or just long enough for the caramel to set.

- Top the cake with a layer of popcorn and a sprinkling of peanuts. With a spoon, drizzle some of the chocolate over the top of the cake. Top with another layer of popcorn, peanuts, and chocolate. Continue making layers until the desired height is achieved. Place the cake in the refrigerator for 15 minutes to firm before serving. Serve any remaining popcorn alongside the cake slices.

Index

Acknowledgments

Working on a book about nothing but popcorn was an interesting experience; one that expanded my culinary knowledge into a completely different realm. Developing and testing some 80 recipes with popcorn as the primary ingredient was fun, comical, and sometimes a bit frustrating.

But, with the help of some associates, we made our way through the task at hand and now present to you popcorn in ways you may have never imagined.

Special thanks to Gary Luke, Rachelle Longé, Rosebud Eustace, and everyone else at Sasquatch Books who provided me the opportunity to write this book.

Thank you again to Gary and to the following folks who helped with recipe testing:

- C-CAP (Career Through Culinary Arts Program), Hampton Roads director Tammy Jaxtheimer, and the following high school students and teachers: Jay Cousin, Ross Glazer, Amy Goodman, Katy Harman, Suzette Johnson, Taneequa Kearney, Kearsta Lau, Lara Naujokas, Natalie Quinn, Leicel Ros, and Blake Sehestedt.
- The following Culinary Institute of Virginia (CIV) students: Gilbert Dawes, J. Brant Lewis, and Jeremy Talley.
- Chef David J. Schneider of For the Culinary Wonders Consulting, Catering & Cooking Lessons of Virginia Beach, Chef Emi Ostrander, and Linda Dyer with daughters Ashley and Liz Dyer.
- Kal and Laura Habr, owners of Croc's 19th Street Bistro in Virginia Beach for hosting a "mass testing" with C-CAP and CIV students, and chefs Greg Hopkins and Nick Aristy for allowing us to mess up their kitchen and leave them with the dirty dishes.

Also, thank you for the wonderful support from Jessica Carlson, Joe Flanagan, Andy Gladstein, Wayne Hylton, Elaine Kennedy, Marisa Marsey, and Melissa Morgan.

About the Author

Patrick Evans-Hylton is a Johnson & Wales University–trained chef, food editor for *Hampton Roads Magazine*, and editor of *Virginia Wine Lover*. He appears weekly on select ABC affiliates with his "Everyday Gourmet" cooking segments. Evans-Hylton is active with Slow Food USA and C-CAP (Career Through Culinary Arts Program), and he is on the board of the International Association of Culinary Professionals.